★U.S. NATIONAL GUARD★

ALWAYS READY, ALWAYS THERE

Carla Mooney

Rourke
Educational Media
rourkeeducationalmedia.com

Scan for Related Titles and
Teacher Resources

www.rourkeeducationalmedia.com

PHOTO CREDITS: Cover photo by Spc. Venessa Hernandez, U.S. Army; back cover and title page flag © SFerdon; Page 4/5 courtesy of National Guard Bureau; Page 6 photo by Sgt. Brandon Aird U.S. Army; Page 7 © Ed Edahl; Pages 8 and courtesy of Library of Congress; Page 10 U.S. Navy photo by Spc. Aaron J. Herrera; Page 11 courtesy of US Air National Guard; Page 12 © Eric Durr; Page 13 photo by Staff Sgt. Andrew Hughan, Sgt. Michael L. Owens; Page 14 photo by Tech. Sgt. David Kujawa; Page 15 courtesy of US National Guard; Page 16 photos by Sgt. Stephen A. Gober, Sgt. John Crosby; Page 17 photos by 2nd Lt. Becky Linder, U.S. Air Force Sgt. Heather Wright; Page 18 © Michael Foran, James Tourtellotte; Page 19 photos by Staff Sgt. Jessica Inigo California National Guard, Andrea Booher/FEMA News Photo; Page 20 photo by Sgt. Doug Roles Pennsylvania National Guard; Page 21 photo by Master Sgt. Kevin J. Gruenwald U.S. Air Force; Page 22 photos by Sgt. Alex C. Sauceda; Page 23 courtesy of US Army, Airman 1st Class Cory D. Payne; Page 24 © Kevin Robertson; Page 25 photos by Sgt Charlie Miller, Staff Sgt. James Wilkinson; Page 26 courtesy of U.S. National Guard, Master Sgt. Jack Braden; Page 27 photos by Maj. Cotton Puryear, Virginia National Guard; Page 29 courtesy of U.S. Navy, Staff Sgt. Blair Heusdens

Edited by Precious McKenzie

Designed and Produced by Blue Door Publishing, FL

Library of Congress Cataloging-in-Publication Data

U.S. National Guard: Always Ready, Always There / Carla Mooney
  p. cm. -- (Freedom Forces)
  ISBN 978-1-62169-928-6 (hard cover) (alk. paper)
  ISBN 978-1-62169-823-4 (soft cover)
  ISBN 978-1-62717-032-1 (e-book)
 Library of Congress Control Number: 2013938880

Also Available as:
ROURKE'S
e-Books

Rourke Educational Media
Printed in the United States of America,
North Mankato, Minnesota

Rourke
Educational Media

rourkeeducationalmedia.com

customerservice@rourkeeducationalmedia.com
PO Box 643328 Vero Beach, Florida 32964

TABLE OF CONTENTS

CHAPTER ONE SERVING COMMUNITY AND COUNTRY

Before the Army, Navy, and Air Force, who protected Americans? As early as 1636, ordinary citizens formed colonial **militias**. Men put down their farming tools and picked up weapons to protect their families and towns from attack. Eventually, these militias became the National Guard.

NATIONAL GUARD

★ ★

ALWAYS READY ALWAYS THERE

The birth of the United States National Guard.

National Guardsman of the 1st Battalion, 151st Infantry Regiment provides security in Parun, Afghanistan.

Today, the National Guard is a reserve military force made up of units from each state and territory. The National Guard serves both the state and federal government. The Guard helps the military in war and the community during disasters. The Guard can also be called to maintain peace and order.

Like ordinary citizens, Guard members live in communities across the country. They work at **civilian** jobs or go to school. They train regularly so that they are ready, wherever and whenever help is needed.

National Guard troops unload supplies to help people after the disaster caused by Hurricane Rita in 2005.

CHAPTER TWO
HISTORY OF THE NATIONAL GUARD

Early American colonists organized groups of men into militias to defend their communities. Colonial militias protected citizens from Native American raids. When the Revolutionary War began, militias fought British soldiers. General George Washington led the militia that volunteered to fight. After battle, militia volunteers were free to go home.

The early American militia were paid, in some cases. Others were offered bounties to stay in service.

After the Revolutionary War, states organized their own militias. State militias sent soldiers to fight during the Mexican War, the Civil War, and the Spanish-American War. In 1903, the U.S. Congress passed a law that joined separate state militias into a single reserve force for the U.S. Army. The force was officially named the National Guard.

Drum Corps, 8th New York State Militia
Arlington, Va., June, 1861

U.S. Soldiers from 214th Military Police Company, Alabama Army National Guard.

National Guard members carry an injured man to a waiting helicopter near the New Orleans Superdome.

Since then, the National Guard has fought in wars worldwide. Guard soldiers fought for America in World Wars I and II, Korea, Vietnam, Iraq, and Afghanistan. After the **terrorist** attacks of September 11, 2001, more than 50,000 Guard members were called to provide security at home and fight terrorism. The Guard also **deployed** troops to help after Hurricane Katrina in 2005. Each day, the National Guard is ready to defend the United States wherever they are needed.

AIR NATIONAL GUARD

In 1947, the Air National Guard was formed. Members of the Air National Guard help their communities and help the U.S. Air Force protect America's skies. The Air National Guard is now part of the U.S. Air Force.

FREEDOM FACT:
In World War II, National Guard units were among the first to deploy overseas and the first to fight.

CHAPTER THREE

JOINING THE GUARD

To join the National Guard, **recruits** must be between 17 and 35 years of age, have a high school education, and be in good physical condition. Recruits must also be U.S. citizens or permanent residents.

Major General Patrick Murphy, the adjutant general of New York, administers the oath of enlistment to six new New York Army National Guard recruits and one New York Air National Guard recruit.

After joining the Guard, like the other military branches, new recruits attend Basic Combat Training (BCT), also known as boot camp. Over a 10-week period, recruits train hard. They wake up before dawn, run, climb walls, and race over **obstacle courses**. They also learn **combat** and weapons skills.

Louisiana Army National Guard student during a training exercise.

Basic training exercises.

After Basic Combat Training, recruits go to Advanced Individual Training (AIT). They receive hands-on training to learn the skills they will need in the Guard. The type of AIT depends on a recruit's job placement. For example, a military intelligence specialist would learn how to interview people or scan pictures from aircraft for information. They would also learn how to prepare and analyze intelligence reports.

Air traffic contoller trainees receive the hands-on portion of their training and gain skills.

After training, Guard members return home. They live, work, or go to school. They attend one drill weekend each month and a two-week training each year. There, Guard members practice military skills so that they are always ready for action.

FREEDOM FACT:
Over 75,000 National Guardsmen were called upon to help bring a swift end to Desert Storm in 1991.

CHAPTER FOUR WORKING IN THE GUARD

There are more than 150 different National Guard jobs. In war, Guard units serve as **infantry,** raid enemy posts, or launch missiles at the enemy. They operate tanks on the battlefield or fly jets in combat. Other Guard members serve as doctors and nurses. Still others work on construction and demolition projects.

Pennsylvania Army National Guard's B Company, 1st Battalion, 111th Infantry, 56th Stryker Brigade Combat Team.

FREEDOM FACT:
There are more than 2,500 National Guard armories worldwide.

Guard members save lives during natural disasters. When Hurricane Katrina struck the Gulf Coast in 2005, the National Guard rescued more than 17,000 people. They helped evacuate 70,000 people out of danger.

NATIONAL GUARD CAREERS

Here is website to find more info on careers:

http://www.nationalguard.com/careers

Potential careers: engineer, infantry, aviation mechanic, communication specialist, military intelligence, military police, transportation specialist, doctor, logistic support, finance manager, interpreter, JAG officer.

Plumes of smoke billow from the World Trade Center towers in New York City after a Boeing 767 hit each tower during the September 11 attacks.

When terrorists attacked the United States on September 11, 2001, the National Guard sprung into action. Guard units dug through the debris of the World Trade Center and searched for survivors. The Air National Guard flew patrols over the country. Other National Guard units patrolled more than 400 of the country's largest airports, setting up security checkpoints.

Guard units patrol borders to stop illegal drugs from entering the country. Others work in counter-terrorism units. All of these jobs are an important part of the National Guard.

Border patrol and the California Guard are working together to secure the state's border.

PEACE KEEPERS

The National Guard may be called for **peacekeeping** duty. In 2002, Guard units kept order at the Salt Lake City Winter Olympics. In 1999, they helped local law enforcement maintain order during the WTO protests in Seattle. The Guard has also traveled to foreign places such as Somalia, Kosovo, and Haiti on peacekeeping missions.

CHAPTER FIVE

HI-TECH GEAR AND VEHICLES

Guard members use many types of equipment. Powerful weapons, such as assault rifles, machine guns, and sniper rifles are used in combat. The Guard is highly trained in safety and accuracy.

The M-16 rifle is a general assault weapon used by many Guard units.

A Utah Army National Guard soldier from the 19th Special Forces is hoisted up to an HH-60 Pave Hawk helicopter.

Guard soldiers rely on state-of-the-art vehicles to carry out missions. They operate tanks and other combat vehicles in battle. These powerful vehicles protect soldiers on the battlefield.

The M1 Abrams tank provides firepower on the battlefield and has heavy armor that protects soldiers.

The Humvee carries troops and weapons over difficult terrain. The Humvee can also be used as an ambulance or in natural disasters.

The AH-64 Apache Longbow helicopter carries missiles and other weapons. It can fly during the day or at night in all weather conditions.

Air National Guard pilots fly many types of aircraft. The C-5 Galaxy is one of the world's biggest planes. It transports people, equipment, and supplies. It can carry a fully equipped combat-ready military unit anywhere in the world. The KC-135 Stratotanker refuels other aircraft in the air. The F-22 Raptor and F-15 Eagle are fighter jets flown in combat.

A KC-135R Stratotanker refuels an F/A-22 Raptor.

C-5 Galaxy

Airmen load the Aviation Combined Arms Tactical Trainer onto a C-5 Galaxy.

The Guard uses high-tech communications equipment. Satellite communications systems allow soldiers to send voice and data messages about real-time conditions during a battle. Commanders use this information to make better battlefield decisions.

Vehicle containing communications equipment that is able to respond to natural disasters or other emergencies.

Guard units are often first to help in an emergency. When needed, the Guard's citizen-soldiers are ready to defend America at a moment's notice.

New satellite systems enable units to communicate and share data all over the world.

TIMELINE

1636:
Colonists organize militias.

1775:
U.S. Army formed.

1917:
The U.S. enters World War I; the National Guard makes up 40 percent of the U.S. combat divisions in France.

1927:
The National Guard provides relief after the great Mississippi flood.

1991:
Operation Desert Storm begins the first Persian Gulf War.

2001:
National Guard units respond to protect America from further terrorist attacks.

1783:
United States defeats Great Britain in American Revolution.

1861-1865:
Civil War.

1903:
National defense legislation increases the role of the National Guard as a reserve force for the U.S. Army.

1941:
The Allies invade Western Europe on D-Day, June 6.

1950-1953:
National Guard units deploy to fight in the Korean War.

1965-1973:
Guard units serve in the Vietnam War.

2003:
U.S. military invades Iraq.

2005:
Hurricane Katrina hits the Gulf Coast; Guard units respond quickly to save lives.

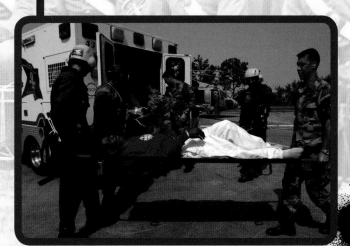

SHOW WHAT YOU KNOW

1. When was the National Guard founded?
2. What are the three basic responsibilities of the National Guard?
3. What is the first training course new Guard recruits take?
4. What are the requirements to join the National Guard?
5. How does the Guard help communities at home?

GLOSSARY

civilian (si-VIL-yuhn): someone who is not a member of the armed forces

combat (KOM-bat): armed fighting with enemy forces

deployed (dih-PLOID): sent troops on a mission or to a battle

infantry (IN-fuhn-tree): the part of an army that fights on the ground

militias (muh-LISH-uhz): groups of citizens who are trained to fight but only serve in an emergency

obstacle courses (OB-stuh-kuhl KORSS-iz): series of barriers that soldiers must jump over, climb, or crawl through

peacekeeping (PEES-kee-ping): military activities to prevent further fighting between countries or groups of people

recruits (ri-KROOTS): new members of the armed forces

terrorist (TER-ur-ist): someone who uses violence and threats to frighten and harm people

Index

Websites to Visit

http://www.goang.com/

http://www.nationalguard.com/

http://www.nationalguard.mil/

About the Author

Carla Mooney has written many books for children and young adults. She lives in Pennsylvania with her husband and three children. She enjoys learning about U.S. history and reading stories of everyday heroes in the National Guard.

Meet The Author!
www.rem4students.com

32